PEARLS

PEARLS

PRACTICAL TIPS FOR ADDING BEAUTY AND VALUE TO YOUR LIFE'S JOURNEY

CARLENE W. LEWIS

Copyright © 2020 by Carlene W. Lewis

All rights reserved.

No part of this book may be reproduced in any form or by any electronic or mechanical means, including information storage and retrieval systems, without written permission from the author, except for the use of brief quotations in a book review.

Disclaimer: This book is the author's own experience and perspectives. The content included is not intended to be a substitute for professional medical advice, diagnosis or treatment. Always seek the advice of a qualified health provider with any questions you may have regarding a specific condition.

For information contact :

Carlene W. Lewis

www.FindingMyElbow.com

Book Cover design by LKB Designs & Photography

Editorial Consult & Interior Design by EvyDani Books, LLC

Editing by Nzadi Amistad

Illustration by Jonathan Barnhill

ISBN: 978-1-7361534-0-6 (paperback)

ISBN: 978-1-7361534-1-3 (ebook)

This book is dedicated to my courageous parents, Henry A. Williams, Jr. and Dorothy C. Williams. To my amazing children, grandchildren, and the broken parts of humanity I've encountered throughout my journey to becoming whole. May your soul work continue until you are no more.

PREFACE

This booklet is the second in the series called *Pearls Along the Path to Destiny*. *Pearls: Book 1* was written during the height of my transition from emotional, physical, psychological, relational, and spiritual bondage. Its contents identified patterns and behaviors of certain dangerous personality types, while providing practical ways to navigate the road to real and sustained liberty.

The most significant aspects of any journey will always have periods of adjustments. With that truth, my offering to those reading this work is to further provide the clarity and insight needed to successfully identify blind spots, make the best choices, and develop a keen awareness of the value of your journey. Just to note, life unfolds in phases. The release of the *Pearls* series will follow suit.

One could argue that a person is responsible for their *own* destiny. But if you walk away leaving that discussion unfinished and unexplored, that approach could garner a lot of frustration. In addition, there could be confusion, anger, and resentment for the poor soul trying to process and digest that oversized serving of truth, minus a clarifier.

PREFACE

The statement is not untrue; it's just not the totality of that which involves fulfilling one's destiny.

Truth could not be found in the pages of this source if I only mentioned destiny without incorporating purpose with the same stroke of the pen. In my opinion, they go hand-in-hand.

Remember, we are not all on the same path, neither are we all here to fulfill the same purpose; as purpose goes…if it were designed in that manner, our existence would be out of balance. For example, we would have all students and no teachers, or we all would be drivers without the benefit of passengers, or we would all be patients without the expertise and knowledge of nurses and doctors.

I acknowledge the fact and am keenly aware that not everyone ascribes to the same faith as I do. However, the information shared here is universal and practical.

This booklet speaks to humanity; therefore, as you read it, consider the treasures within them and apply the wisdom of its content. You will find the divide narrows exponentially between the reader and writer when the realization of purpose and destiny is experienced.

So, settle yourselves in for a brief read of insightful, explosive, and practical information that will explain, expound, and empower you, the reader. The *choice* is yours! Pick up the pearls and add them to your strand or leave them for someone else.

CONSTRUCTS: THE FRAMEWORK OF YOUR SOUL

A part of maturation and growth requires us to identify what we believe about ourselves, our surroundings, our experiences, and our desires. Doing so will allow us to expand our ability to correctly filter those experiences and perceptions.

This one definition of construct resonated with me. According to changingminds.org:

> "People develop internal models of reality called <u>constructs</u> to understand and explain the world around them in the same way that scientists develop theories. Like scientists, they develop these constructs based on observation and experimentation. Constructs, thus, start as unstable conjecture, changing and stabilizing as more experience and proof is gained. When constructs are challenged or incomplete, the result is emotional states such as anxiety, confusion, anger, and fear."

When we are faced with the challenge to change, grow, and expand, it then becomes a pivotal point at the intersection called choice. It is at this intersection that personal and internal constructs must be examined.

I want you, the reader, to consider these five constructs. If you examine them from a posture of truth, you have consciously positioned yourself to make informed choices about yourself, your environment, your experiences, and so forth. There is no right or wrong answer. It is yours to own, reject, modify, or destroy. So, take a moment and answer these as honestly as you can.

FOUNDATIONAL CONSTRUCTS

- Who are you?
- Whose imprint is on your soul? Who has impacted your beliefs about yourself the most?
- What do you believe about yourself?
- When was the last time your visual filter was upgraded?
- Are you open and willing to examine your perspectives?

CHOICE

I want to reiterate that, although we have the power of *choice*, the fullness of what that means will be different for everyone. Just know, this is perfectly fine. As we explore the predicament called choice, many considerations must be afforded to individuality.

This booklet is not written to define what your considerations should be but, rather, to remind you of the power that lies within them. This includes the power to choose and embrace the beauty of life with all its complications. A simple working definition of choice is: The ability to select or decide when faced with two or more possibilities with a corresponding action.

Choice is the anchoring cord, *the start of the strand*, if you will, which secures the corresponding actions of your "pearls." Choosing to become a participant in the direction of your life's journey is the most important decision you will ever make. The addition of this *pearl* called choice is vital!

Generally, and in theory, (most) humans have the capacity and privilege of choice! But having the capacity and privilege is only the beginning. What we do with that privilege and capacity is a key component to how we live and leave this earth.

POWER PEARL

Choice is a provision that we, for the most part, have at our fingertips, and when it is given serious considerations, the trajectory changes, the landscape changes, and the perspective changes.

I see choice as an artist's initial sketch. The initial sketch outlines an idea, which allows the artist to capture certain hints of an idea that is being formulated. When we decide to use choice for growth, sometimes, it is the beginning concept of the space we are in at that given tine. But it is not the whole masterpiece!

Like the artist's initial sketch, it lends itself to direction, and that direction lends itself to a plan, and that plan provides a visual, and that visual defines the necessary strategy for completion of the artist's idea.

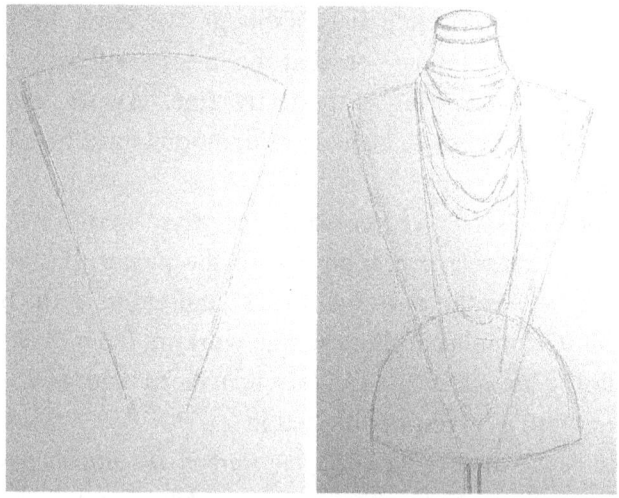

Choice must become the foundational push for positive change. Because choice can be incremental, there may not be immediate evidence of its impact. Choice, just like the artist's initial sketch, is not always well-defined. As the artist's concept or idea unfolds, much like choice, sometimes, the lines become distorted or worn thin to the point of holes because of the need to erase repeatedly, often, in the same spot, trying desperately to make the parts align and capture the concept! The power of choice allows one to reset, change, and try again until the concept becomes visible.

Having the privilege of choice does not eliminate disappointments, setbacks, emotional pain, rejection, betrayals, intimidation, fear, loss of focus, failures, humiliation, doubt, trauma, death of loved ones, loss of friendships, financial disasters, and disarray. Life happens with or without your decision to plug in.

How we choose to use this privilege called choice defines the masterpiece of our existence! It illuminates our imprint upon others who are in our space. It also magnifies the essence of our legacy, or the lack thereof, for generations to come.

PEARL OF TRUTH

How unfair, negligent, unrealistic, and unsympathetic my message would be if I failed to acknowledge and discuss certain facts? There are certain circumstances in this life that dictate, mandate, crush, and pigeon-hole our *choices! PERIOD.* One of these circumstances is our interaction with the influencers in our lives.

Influencers are specific people in our lives who impact the choices we make. They can be our parents, grandparents, husbands, wives, children, uncles, bosses, pastors, siblings, teachers, etc. In other words, our influencers can occupy key positions in our lives. Their character can be honest and loving. Or they can have a manipulative and unkind soul. It is important for you to discern who will be allowed to stand in your space as an influencer.

One important point to consider is that the weight and heaviness of harmful imprints can determine the depth and focus required of you to fight for the privilege of choice. The power of your choice has a *signature,* one which travels with you for a lifetime and even beyond your lifetime. Choice can grant life, liberty, empowerment, change, and growth. Choice also has the power to mitigate poverty cycles, abusive cycles, poor physical health cycles, and so on. It holds destiny and purpose in itself! What a gift!

POWER PEARL

A skillful artist does not develop overnight. Nor does their creative work develop into a masterpiece overnight. Similarly, neither do the sketches of our lives.

Although the sketch does not define what the finished piece will look like, in the end, there are indelible strokes which frame us. The sketch will take on many forms and shapes before it is refined and can be appreciated as art.

Ultimately, we are responsible for our choices. I believe choice and all the dimensions of it are like pencils in the hands of the artist. Each line, each direction, every stroke, and movement are essential to the process. The art of shading for depth and definition, every irritating erasure and correction, all of it, lends itself to completion, to alignment, to beauty, and to the purpose of the artist's masterpiece.

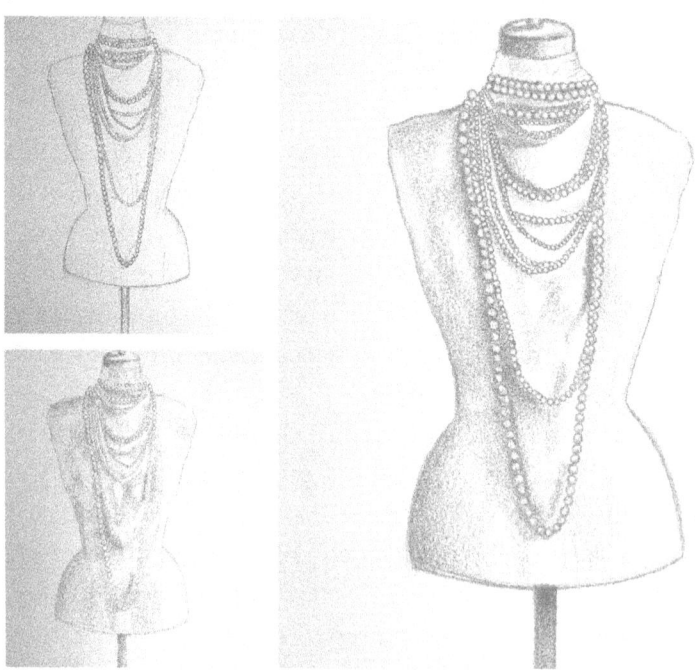

ACTION PEARL

There are serious questions you must ask yourself when you are faced with choices. The ones I have included below are not in order of importance, but the weight and order of importance lay within the bounty of your actions, inactions, or reactions. Let us dive into the questions:

- Will the imprint of our lives be appreciated?
- Will the conversations express gratitude for having known us?
- Will our imprint evoke smiles or sadness?
- Will our imprint be erratic and inconsistent?
- Will the memory be unforgettable and exact?
- Can one be found discussing the moment your imprint, your sketch, propelled them into the choice of being free?
- Will they say your imprint challenged and changed their perspective?
- Will they say you cared?
- Will it show shared ideas with others, which provided life-changing contributions?
- Will our families, friends, colleagues, and those we are destined to meet remember our positive life force and energy for generations to come?
- Will our life imprints, tracks, and snapshots be easily washed away by a light drizzle of rain?
- Will our life imprints be carelessly tossed in an obscure section of a drawer rarely opened?

As I reflect on my own destiny, purpose, legacy, contributions, and presence on this Earth, I must ask myself, will it only be a snapshot of a one-dimensional existence? Or will it involve a running video which holds an array of snapshots that are pertinent for my journey and those who are destined to meet me? The fact is, fulfilling one's destiny and purpose does not rest entirely in our choice, but rather the **God** or **gods** of our choices.

JOURNEY

In my work, I use the term *journey* frequently. You see, our lives represent the epitome of what a journey is. Life, in one of its many aspects, can be described as traveling from one place to another, not specific to the notion of a physical location, but ultimately and literally evolving, developing, growing, and learning to travel prepared, all while experiencing the many intricacies of this living force of energy called life. This is what I know about journeying; it must be preceded with a decision (choice), a goal (action), and the tools (insight) needed to journey prepared.

PEARL OF TRUTH

Each of us will have our own journey. While our journeys may be similar, it is of utmost importance that you remember that your journey is your own. As such, you cannot measure your journey against someone else's.

POWER PEARL

Each of our journeys begins with the decision called choice. It is up to you to choose how your journey will progress. Throughout life, we are faced with various situations. The variations can drive the trajectory of the journey; however, it's up to you to make the best choice that will place you in the best space for your journey.

ACTION PEARL

The activation of your journey will happen when you are able to identify where you are currently. Are you broken? Healing? Hopeful? Your journey has to begin somewhere, and knowing honestly and truthfully where you are can be the compass that is needed for safe passage.

AWARENESS

*A*wareness is such a powerful position to occupy. Awareness holds within itself beautiful answers, understanding, recognition, strategy, and resolutions. Being aware of who you are, where you are, and where you will journey positions you for greatness. Awareness brings you to an uncomplicated place within yourself. It also gives you permission to be who you were created to be. Awareness is a springboard for change and choice. Awareness will not always present itself easily. Life has a way of cluttering us to the point of pushing or giving away the greatness we possess.

We can often recognize the greatness inside of us, but there is no outlet. There is no tribe or village to help you realize your greatness. Then, there is the potential of becoming stuck. Being *aware* of who's sharing your space and who should be sharing your space is vital. Not knowing (being unaware) can hinder your journey to your purpose and destiny. Listen carefully — greatness has its own place setting. It is not defined by the masses. It springs forth in the midst of the most mundane things.

There are two personality types I will discuss as it relates to awareness. There's the *theorist* and the *explorer*. They both possess the desire to have answers. But their processes, at some point, take a sharp turn, rendering one with "the goods" and the other with a process for "potentially getting the goods." Don't get stuck on your journey. Remember *awareness* gifts you with strategy.

The explorer is willing to fail, to fall, to be rejected, to seem foolish, to be alone, to invest personal finances, to go into debt, and to have doubt, but the explorer makes moves anyway. The explorer is willing to be humiliated, to be fearful, and to be embarrassed. The explorer is often labeled a fool and risks their physical life to find that which is being sought after! These are but a few hurdles the explorer experiences.

The theorist is cautious. Their job requires the *consideration* of facts. They spend their lives observing, contemplating, comparing, and reasoning to prove or disprove a given theory. An interesting note: the theorist must follow a strict set of established guidelines when developing a theory, only to prove or disprove the theory works. The explorer, however, is aware of the risks involved and is willing to take them! A key to reaching greatness is choosing to take the risk anyway.

Let's look at some obstacles you may face on your journey. They can be personal, professional, ministerial, financial, familial, emotional, and even physical. They can also be complicated and dangerous. They may have layers, trap doors, misinformation, unexpected illnesses, and even death. Some long-held beliefs and traditions can also become obstacles. Whatever the barriers, the explorer is willing to proceed because he is *aware* of how important his journey is.

The explorer (purpose pursuer) will not completely yield to the barriers created by opposition. Although bewildered and overwhelmed at times, the explorer rarely gives up. The explorer has an unyielding desire to "ask" one more time, "seek" one more time, "knock" one more time, "pray" one more time, "preach" one more time, "believe" one more time, "give" one more time, "love" one more time, "worship" one more time, "sing" a new song one more time, "write" one more time, "show up" one more time, "forgive" one more time, "call" one more time, "apply" one more time, "dance" one more time, "trust" one more time, "get up" one more time, and "serve" just one more time!

Much like the explorer, those of us who fall within this category believe that, from the foundation of the world, a seed was dropped into the nutrient-rich soil of their soul, that inner self, the part which leads us to seek out and discover purpose or die trying. And in that discovery, we are able to skillfully weave into the fabric of our journey the divine seed which yields its purpose and ultimately escorts and creates the space for The Kingdom of God to be revealed on Earth, in our lives, in our families, our ministries, marketplaces, and for generations to come, as it is in heaven.

PEARL OF TRUTH

Once you become aware of yourself (self-awareness) that awareness allows for a shift in perspective. It changes your mindset (changes how you typically live your life).

POWER PEARL

Awareness is such a powerful gift! It elevates your vantage point, helps you to identify that which is good for you, and that which is not. Awareness is the gift that keeps on giving!

ACTION PEARL

Awareness is different for different people. It's a space of discovery. You have permission to keep what you like about yourself and work on areas you don't like about yourself. Awareness gives you the gift to strategically command a space. It's a power tool for us to use as a means of leverage. There is nothing more powerful than knowing your strengths and weaknesses!

DISCOVERY

There is an important question you must be able to answer. That is "Who are you?" The answer cannot be an afterthought. And it must be answered in its purest form without hesitation. If you cannot admit to and/or be truthful about who you are, others will. When you see yourself through a truthful lens, this allows space for change, and it empowers you to denounce and dismiss those who will assign your identity to you!

SELF

So, let's look at the definition of self. According to Lexico.com (which is a collaboration with Oxford Dictionary hosted by Dictionary.com), *"a person's essential being that distinguishes them from others, especially considered as the object of introspection or reflexive action."* Listen, having and/or developing a created space in your soul to allow for positive transformations against negative attributes is essential.

An unwillingness to face the real you (self) is a clear indicator of immaturity. As you may well know, immaturity stunts your ability to grow and expand in most areas of your life.

Although the question "who are you?" deserves an answer, it is not the most important question to answer right now, not yet...

ME

For such a small word, its depth is boundless. It's so boundless in fact, we all have had a personal experience with the elements of the word *me*. I know you're asking, is there a different meaning for the words *self* and *me*? I believe so. They are used interchangeably, but there are differences. This is how I see the two. The word *self* is more sophisticated at its base than the word *me* is. *Self* includes many internal facets of development, such as identifying, filtering, rejecting, receiving, accepting, assessing, revisiting, planting, awareness, courage, insight, pulling close to the positive, and rejecting the negative. Whereas the word *me* stands as the mold from which *self* has carved out for you! *Self* empowers *me* to walk it out!

Ask yourself this question, "What does knowing *me* have to do with purpose and destiny?" You see, inside the word *me* is your lifetime (i.e. *self*).

Built by the process of self-awareness, *me* is a compilation of your soul's series. As a child, I remember my Big Momma (Addie Bell Chappell) having an old trunk. It was dated and worn, but at some point, it was once new! It served a purpose until it didn't anymore. There was all kinds of stuff in it. I was too young to be specific, but old enough to understand it held meaningful things!

This is how I imagine *me* in its full form, holding *meaningful things*, *self* built. It's filled with photos, snapshots, seeds, branches, leaves, blossoms, levels, love, layers, open doors, thorns, dust, memories, dirt, hate, spider webs, locked doors, gold, dreams, goals, ideals, experiences, and love.

UNDERSTANDING ME

The assessment of me is necessary for truth. When we lack basic and necessary intimacy with ourselves, this weakens our ability to rightly discern our surroundings. This makes us vulnerable to those who invade our space, our psyche, and our soul. We, then, become vulnerable, stationary targets, waiting to be taken down.

I must admit, being acquainted with your *me* is most difficult for females, in general, and black females, in particular. To add to that group is a sub-group of black females whose upbringing was religious in nature and defined by a patriarchal set of values.

Realistically, this sub-group rarely has the leisure to define *me*. Most often, their world is cluttered with tasks, unaddressed traumas, unrealistic responsibilities, and so on. You see, the healthy outcome of knowing *me* propels you onto the path of truth. The truth that is required to define *me* also serves as a vehicle which allows us to experience truth in all areas of our lives.

If you have discovered your *me*, this discovery is priceless. This knowledge repels others who may attempt to deceive and devalue you. Having this knowledge is immeasurable. It's akin to having tools and materials that answer problems. It's like wearing armor or being a skilled detective. You can quickly dismiss those areas not suited for you.

Your *me* resides in the comfort of intimacy, intimacy on a profoundly deep level, which few have experienced. You see, once *me* has been discovered, it becomes very difficult for you to entertain fools. Discovering your true *me* is inexplicably tied to knowing your purpose. How can there be an identification of purpose without having a deep knowledge of your *me*?

PEARL OF TRUTH

"This above all: to thine own self be true and it must follow, as the night the day, thou canst not then be false to any man." (William Shakespeare) Power comes with knowing who you are.

POWER PEARL

Access is not far from you when you become one with your *me*.

ACTION PEARL

You must silence yourself. The unhealthy imprints, opinions, histories, and experiences must be laid to rest. When you silence yourself, you, then, must be willing to accept what is there or change it. There will always be voices, working to disturb your journey. Knowing your *me* has the power of sight, you must be prepared for the journey.

DESTINY & PURPOSE

The words *destiny* and *purpose* are often used interchangeably. For the sake of our work together, I want to make sure that we clearly understand the definitions of destiny and purpose. In fact, I want you to understand their distinct differences and how they work together when activated in our lives.

Destiny and purpose are a shared feeling. It is known among those who have learned to listen to it and for it. It is shared with those who are in the realm of agreement that you are placed on this earth for divine reasons. There is a common thread that runs deeply through those of us who desire to meet destiny and purpose in person. You shouldn't just toy with the theory of destiny and purpose only to appear aware. But you should want to be acutely aware of the glory associated with identifying your life's purpose and fulfilling destiny.

DESTINY

Destiny is the space where you were born. We were released into this realm for a specific walk. Each person's destiny is different. Destiny does not mean high socio-economic standing, academic excellence, pop-culture acknowledgement and acceptance, local popularity, a world-wide known ministry with accolades and so on. In its most basic sense, destiny can be described as the fulfillment of your essence. With that fulfillment being executed in a real and practical way, lives are changed (including yours) for God's glory and your satisfaction.

PURPOSE

Purpose is the catalyst that is needed for destiny to happen. When you operate in your purpose, every stage or phase of purpose drives you closer to your destiny. Purpose is the automobile, a vehicle whose motion is driving you to destiny.

You meet destiny by walking the path that has been assigned to you. Ultimately, when purpose and destiny collide, you have success. That's why it is necessary for you to identify and operate in it.

PEARL OF TRUTH

We have to go back to choice. The appropriate actions will put you smack dab in the middle of finding your purpose, so you can reach destiny.

POWER PEARL

Once you have engaged in purpose, you can't be easily led astray. Know that it is your make up, and no one can buy or take that away from you. Destiny and purpose are profound in that they allow you to impact people's lives in ways you could never imagine. The reach of your influence will be realized for generations to come. The fulfillment of destiny and purpose positions you for success. No one can steal or take away your birthright. No one can take the lesson or moment away. There is power in walking your purpose out. Being in purpose and destiny causes those in your circle to shift. It provides them with a choice to do something different. There is revelation in destiny and purpose.

ACTION PEARL

Activating destiny and purpose in your life happens one step at a time. The steps include having the following:

- A village of common/likeminded folk
- Accountability
- Persistence

It's time to take the first step. Then another. And another…

A CIRCLE BACK TO CHOICE

Choice, in its most basic form, is theoretically a privilege every person is given. And each person has the ability to activate it and journey well. This unfortunately is not the entire truth as mentioned in the preface. But there's a hidden gem within the layers of choice. That hidden gem possesses a strand which is built upon value systems that are driven by belief systems, which ultimately create triumph or defeat. Conversely, your active participation in finding the gem is essential.

The foundation of journeying prepared is directly affected by the health of our emotional selves and our souls. Healing in these areas is not optional. You choosing to invest in soul care and self-care work go hand in hand with choice. You must always choose and strive to be in optimal health, both physical. as well as emotionally. I will caution you again, there is no comparing your optimal to another's.

One of my favorite scriptures states: *"For I know the thoughts and plans that I have for you, says the Lord, thoughts and plans for welfare and peace and not for evil, to give you hope in your final outcome"* (Jeremiah 29:11). That's a beautiful promise and truth. Again, this is my belief system, my anchoring strand. Yours may not look like mine, but this truth is: You must be able to identify your anchoring strand and hold on to it. we have pearls to gather and display.

When we finally believe, we have value and our choices become congruent with our beliefs. Our movement is different. Our perspectives about *self* and *me* change, and the way we process the hands we were dealt also changes.

As we build the anchoring cord of our strand to hang our pearls on, I want to remind you that your anchoring cord should possess the framework of your soul, healthy constructs from which to work from, an awareness of you, choices, your journey, discovery, then purpose and destiny. What a beautiful display this will make.

One of the single, most important points I will make in this booklet is this: Before destiny and purpose and vision and calling is sought after, you must first pursue the foundation of a healed soul, coupled with healed emotions and a healed psyche. Without successfully addressing these areas, your choices, that powerful privilege, is in danger of being destructive at its base.

The pervasive danger of a person who has a platform of any kind, minus the foundation of self-regulation, emotional wellness, soul health, which is anchored with healthy coping skills, can be compared to an insidious, unknown plague affecting and infecting each person it meets.

This is what I know. My anchoring cord is mine to possess. And my choice to possess it is rewarding. The value of my anchoring cord can never be measured. Nor can it be duplicated. The expression of each experience has shaped, formed, refined, rejected, repelled, battled, and accepted the beauty of the pearls which are found hanging on my anchoring cord. Above all, my prayer, my desire is that you will find value in your anchoring cord and you possess it and proudly display it for the world to see, as you fulfill purpose and destiny.

ACKNOWLEDGMENTS

A special thanks to those who have been instrumental in my healing process, growth, and expansion. My maturation and liberty have been furthered by your support.

ABOUT THE AUTHOR

Carlene W. Lewis is a native of Union Springs, Alabama. A Registered Nurse by vocation, Carlene has extensive management and practice in the area of mental health and psychiatric nursing. Carlene is also an ordained Elder which allows the spiritual component necessary for holistic nursing to flow with ease, thereby treating the whole person. Her mission is simple - to serve as a catalyst for healing and restoration of the injured soul (essence/self) through soul care.

Carlene uses writing as a tool for expression. She is a songwriter and the author of *Pearls Along the Pathway to Destiny*. She is the mother of four and "BaBa" of five grandchildren.

www.ingramcontent.com/pod-product-compliance
Lightning Source LLC
Chambersburg PA
CBHW031309060426
42444CB00032B/897